THE NETHER

THE NETHER

⊰ A PLAY ⊱

JENNIFER HALEY

NORTHWESTERN UNIVERSITY PRESS

EVANSTON, ILLINOIS

Northwestern University Press
www.nupress.northwestern.edu

LIBRARY OF CONGRESS
CATALOGING-IN-PUBLICATION DATA

Haley, Jennifer, author.
  The nether : a play / Jennifer Haley.
    pages cm
  Includes bibliographical references.
  ISBN 978-0-8101-3063-0 (pbk. : alk. paper) — ISBN 978-0-8101-3064-7 (ebook)
    I. Title.
  PS3608.A5464N48 2014
  812.6—dc23
                              2014033200

♾ The paper used in this publication meets the minimum requirements of the American National Standard for Information Sciences—Permanence of Paper for Printed Library Materials, ANSI Z39.48-1992.

For Neel

CONTENTS

PRODUCTION HISTORY

The Nether had its world premiere on March 24, 2013, at the Kirk Douglas Theatre in Los Angeles, California, produced by Center Theatre Group (Michael Ritchie, artistic director; Edward L. Rada, managing director; Douglas C. Baker, producing director; Nausica Stergiou, general manager). It was directed by Neel Keller, with scenic design by Adrian W. Jones, costume design by Alex Jaeger, lighting design by Christopher Kuhl, and sound design by John Zalewski. The cast was as follows:

Sims . . . . Robert Joy
Doyle . . . . Dakin Matthews
Morris . . . . Jeanne Syquia
Woodnut . . . . Adam Haas Hunter
Iris . . . . Brighid Fleming

The Nether received its European premiere on July 17, 2014, at the Royal Court Theatre, London, in a co-production between Headlong (Jeremy Herrin, artistic director; Henny Finch, executive producer) and the Royal Court Theatre (Vicky Featherstone, artistic director; Lucy Davies, executive producer). It was directed by Jeremy Herrin, with set design by Es Devlin, costume design by Christina Cunningham, lighting design by Paul Pyant, sound design by Ian Dickinson, original music by Nick Powell, and video design by Luke Halls. The cast was as follows:

Sims . . . . Stanley Townsend
Doyle . . . . David Beames
Morris . . . . Amanda Hale
Woodnut . . . . Ivanno Jeremiah
Iris . . . . Zoe Brough/Isabella Pappas

THE NETHER

CHARACTERS

Sims/Papa, a successful businessman
Morris, a young female detective
Doyle, a middle-aged science teacher
Iris, a shining little girl
Woodnut, a fresh-faced guest

Time Period: Soon

Setting: An interrogation room and the Hideaway

Nether realm

1. Another world for mythical creatures
2. Demon world
3. A dimension of Evil or Imagination
—*urbandictionary.com*

SCENE 1
INTERROGATION ROOM

[SIMS *sits across a wide table from* DETECTIVE MORRIS.]

SIMS: I want to go home.

MORRIS: Which home?

SIMS: I need to speak with my family.

MORRIS: Which family?

SIMS: I don't know what you're getting at. I want my phone call.

MORRIS: There are things we want, too.

SIMS: My lawyer.

MORRIS: Which lawyer?

SIMS: Come on!

MORRIS: You are free to contact whomever you wish, Mr. Sims. We have a terminal here if you'd care to log in.

SIMS:

MORRIS: I imagine your wife is worried by now.

SIMS: Leave her out of this.

MORRIS: Your children.

SIMS: I don't have any children.

MORRIS: You have a beautiful home, Mr. Sims. Victorian. Set back from a country lane. Children on the front porch in long stockings and sailor caps. Barnaby. Donald. Antonia. Iris. Such quaint names. From an era associated with . . . innocence.

SIMS: I have a brownstone. My wife is sterile. You've got the wrong guy.

MORRIS [consulting a report]: Solicitation. Rape. Sodomy. Murder. These are heavy charges, Mr. Sims.

SIMS: Are you charging me?

MORRIS: The repetitive nature of the offenses. The amount of money you've made.

SIMS: If you're not charging me—

MORRIS: We know about your account in Burkina Faso.

SIMS: If you're not charging me, you have to let me—

MORRIS: Oh, you're free to go.

SIMS: I'm free to go?

MORRIS: We can't hold you here without charging you. That would be against the law.

SIMS: Okay. Then I'm going to go.

MORRIS: We can't control a person's body. Yours is free to walk out the door.

SIMS: Great. My body is walking out the door.

MORRIS: But if it does, we'll rescind your login, Mr. Sims. You will never have access to a terminal again.

SIMS [*slight pause*]: Who did you say you are?

MORRIS: This is an investigative unit of the Nether. I am an in-world representative. My name is Detective Morris.

SIMS: I have business in the Nether. All of my connections. You can't expel me.

MORRIS: You have a taste for the old-fashioned. Think of it as a return to simpler times.

SIMS: This is a violation of my rights. My lawyers are the best in the field. You won't keep me out for long.

MORRIS: Long enough to locate and detain your children.

SIMS:

MORRIS: What's wrong, Mr. Sims?

SIMS:

MORRIS: I thought you didn't have any children.

SIMS:

MORRIS: We sent someone undercover to your realm to make sure our charges were grounded. Because you've programmed it so that nothing there may be recorded, he submitted a written report.

[*consulting a report*] After undergoing a meticulous security scan of my login, creating my character from a set of prescribed looks, and passing a Draconian manners tutorial dissuading modern terminology, I enter the Hideaway.

The first thing I experience is the trees. The flickering light and soft sound as they sway in the sun and wind is almost overwhelming. They surround a beautifully rendered 1880s Gothic Revival with a squeak in the top porch step. I ring the doorbell. I can actually feel my hand sweat, clutching my carpetbag. I peek through a window and spy figures in the foyer—an impeccably dressed man stroking the face of one of the children, a little girl—

SIMS: They. Are not. Children.

MORRIS: I guess that depends on context, Mr. Sims. Or should I call you—Papa?

SCENE 2
INTERROGATION ROOM

[DOYLE *sits across the table from* MORRIS, *head in his hands.*]

MORRIS: Mr. Doyle?

DOYLE:

MORRIS: Mr. Doyle.

DOYLE:

MORRIS: Mr. Doyle, we have not told your wife.

[DOYLE *raises his head.*]

At this point we are merely detaining you. We need information about this man called Papa. In exchange, we will protect your identity.

[*consulting a report*] Cedric Doyle. You are a teacher at Franklin Middle School. You won a Distinguished Teaching Award in Science. You are one year away from retirement with full pension for forty years service in the school district. Your wife is a senior vestry member of St. Thomas Episcopal Church, where you used to teach Sunday school until about four years ago. You have one daughter, a junior at Illinois State.

[*looking up*] Footing the bill for an in-world college. That's a huge expense, Mr. Doyle. Most students now get their higher education at online institutions in the Nether. You claim to moonlight as a professor at one of these institutions—the [*consulting the report*] University of Metaphysical Certitude.

If you like, this entire story about who you are may remain intact. We've even made arrangements with UMC to actually hire you. All those hours at your terminal, plus the boost in your bank account, will continue to make perfect sense.

DOYLE: May I keep her?

MORRIS: Keep who?

DOYLE: Iris.

MORRIS: No, Mr. Doyle. Once we have what we need on Papa, that life is over.

DOYLE:

MORRIS:

DOYLE: I have nothing to say.

SCENE 3
INTERROGATION ROOM

[MORRIS *and* SIMS.]

SIMS: What authority do you have, yanking me from my garden?

MORRIS: We thought face-to-face interaction would be a good change for you.

SIMS: You shouldn't even know who I am. I have the right to remain anonymous.

MORRIS: We're able to track most of our users, but your identity encryption is like nothing we've ever seen. Once you log in, you disappear.

SIMS: Are you pissed you can't target me for advertising?

MORRIS: We don't care about you, Mr. Sims. It's your realm. The Hideaway. Have you heard of obscenity laws?

SIMS: My realm is properly registered and meets all international requirements.

MORRIS: What about your server?

SIMS: My server?

MORRIS: The physical machine where you store the code for the Hideaway.

SIMS: Yes, I know what it is.

MORRIS: We want to know its location.

SIMS: I don't have to tell you that.

MORRIS: I suggest that you do.

SIMS: My server is not in this country. So it's not any of your business.

MORRIS: Your content is here. Your content is everywhere.

SIMS: It's not in your jurisdiction.

MORRIS: Mr. Sims, wherever your content appears is my jurisdiction.

SIMS:

MORRIS: Your realm is not only popular, but lucrative. It's afforded you [*consulting a report*] two hundred square feet of real grass, surrounding your brownstone. A garden of snap peas and swiss chard. Your wife's clothes are made from cotton. Why, with such in-world abundance, do you choose the life of a shade?

SIMS: I'm not a shade.

MORRIS: Your login records indicate you spend a great deal of time online.

SIMS: You have a lot of work on your hands if that's become a crime.

MORRIS: So you've never considered crossing over?

SIMS: I maintain my in-world life. I tend my garden.

MORRIS: But really, Mr. Sims, an average of sixteen hours a day in the Nether? What can be gained by spending so much time in something that isn't real?

SIMS: Just because it's virtual doesn't mean it isn't real. Eighty percent of the population work in office realms, children attend school in educational realms. There's a realm for anything you want to know or do or think you might want to try. As the Nether becomes our contextual framework for being, don't you think it's a bit out of date to say it isn't real?

MORRIS: Is your wife aware of your tendencies?

SIMS: She asks no questions as long as the wine-made-from-grapes arrives at the door.

MORRIS: Your tendencies toward children, Mr. Sims.

SIMS [*slight pause*]: Like everyone, she's as aware as she wants to be.

MORRIS: What if we made her very aware?

SIMS: I expect she would resent you.

MORRIS: Or brought it to the attention of your neighbors?

SIMS: I don't spend enough time in-world to worry about my standing in the community. And my record is whistle clean. Real children are hard to come by these days. It's not like they play outside anymore.

MORRIS: Are you trying to be droll, Mr. Sims?

SIMS: Yeah, I'm trying very hard to be very fucking droll.

MORRIS: It won't reflect well on your case.

SIMS: Do I have a case here? A case sounds legal, which this definitely is not.

MORRIS: We need you to give us the location of your server. When we have confiscated your hardware and deleted your realm, you'll be free to go without prosecution—

SIMS: This is against the law!

MORRIS: Relax, Mr. Sims.

SIMS: My realm is clearly designated Adult. There are adults behind the children and adults behind the guests. My background checks are thorough in the extreme to make sure we don't involve users who are underage. This is in accordance with the statute on consensual roleplay—

MORRIS: You seem to be quite up on laws and statutes.

SIMS: This is my business—

MORRIS: This is our business, too. The Nether is home to many businesses, with an obligation to protect the needs of our community. And our community has decided that realms such as yours are impermissable—

SIMS [*sarcastic*]: Was there a vote?

MORRIS: Yes, there was. I suggest you pay greater attention to the message boards.

SIMS: This is shit. You're feeding me shit.

MORRIS: Would you care to log in right now and check?

SIMS: So you can trace me to my server? No, I would not.

MORRIS: Then you'll just have to trust I'm telling the truth.

SIMS: Trust you? Who are you?!

MORRIS: The Nether is no longer some great Wild West. We have a political body that is just as real as anything in-world. And we're making our own laws, with our own form of prosecution. You ask what authority I have? Look around. There's no Hideaway here. Now I suggest you sit down.

SIMS:

MORRIS:

SIMS: Look, Detective, I am sick. I am sick and have always been sick and there is no cure. No amount of cognitive behavioral therapy or relapse determent or even chemical castration will sway me from my urges toward children. I am sick and no matter how much I loved him or her I would make my own child sick and I see this, I see this—not all of us see this—but I have been cursed with both compulsion and insight. I have taken responsibility for my sickness. I am protecting my neighbor's children and my brother's children and the children I won't allow myself to have, and the only way I can do this is because I've created a place where I can be my fucking self!

SCENE 4
THE HIDEAWAY FOYER, THE NETHER

[*A ray of sunlight beams through a tall window.* PAPA *enters as* IRIS *runs in, breathless. He catches her, spins her around in the light. She shrieks with laughter. He puts her down, and she wobbles in circles.*]

IRIS: Whoa! I'm a top!

PAPA: Was that fun?

IRIS: Yes! I feel dizzy!

PAPA: I thought you'd like that. It's new.

IRIS: Have you given it a name?

PAPA: Not yet. Any ideas?

IRIS: I'd call it the Spinning Top.

PAPA: The Spinning Top it is.

IRIS: Did you try it on Barnaby?

PAPA: You're the first.

IRIS: I am?

PAPA: I knew you'd appreciate it the most. I need an easy audience to give me heart.

IRIS [*suggestively*]: Are you saying I'm easy?

PAPA: Now Iris . . . that joke is too old for you.

[*She giggles and reassumes innocence.*]

IRIS: I've never asked you for anything, have I, Papa?

PAPA: No, you haven't.

IRIS: I was thinking. I might want a birthday party.

PAPA: A birthday party?

IRIS: Yes.

PAPA: Are you trying to grow up? You're already nine years old.

IRIS: I imagined the yard dressed in streamers. And birthday cake. We could invite our favorite Hideaway guests.

PAPA: Involve the guests. So this is an entrepreneurial idea?

IRIS: Somewhat.

PAPA: Somewhat?

IRIS: Not altogether.

PAPA: Then what? You must tell me what's on your mind.

IRIS: I want a day that's all about me.

PAPA:

IRIS:

PAPA: Come here.

[*She moves to him.*]

We have a beautiful home here, Iris. We have a beautiful family, of which you are an important member. It is this beauty which draws our guests. And of course a sympathetic community. But do you know what is the most important thing we offer? [*She shakes her head.*] An opportunity to live outside of consequence. [*She thinks this over.*] Nothing here can change. Which is a beautiful reflection of the way we are changeless.

IRIS: Like the way God sees us.

PAPA: God?

IRIS [*almost guiltily*]: I've been thinking about God.

PAPA: I see.

IRIS: Not as in a person. But as in the way we are with each other. Do you think about God that way?

[*The sound of a grand doorbell is heard.*]

PAPA: We have a guest. You'd best go to the parlor.

IRIS: Yes, Papa.

[*She turns to go.*]

PAPA: Iris? I'm sorry we cannot have a birthday. It would upset a balance here to suggest you're growing older.

IRIS: I understand.

PAPA: I know you do. You're my darling girl.

[PAPA *puts his hand to her cheek.* WOODNUT *enters, and* PAPA *quickly drops his hand. He gives* IRIS *a gentle push, and she exits.* PAPA *turns to* WOODNUT.]

PAPA: My good sir! Welcome to the Hideaway!

WOODNUT: Thank you!

PAPA: Your first time?

WOODNUT: As a matter of fact, yes. Is it obvious?

PAPA: Not to worry. Keep coming back and you'll fit right in.

WOODNUT: You're confident I'll wish to return?

PAPA: I guarantee it, Mr. . . .

WOODNUT: Woodnut. Thomas Woodnut. And you are . . . ?

PAPA: You may call me Papa.

SCENE 5
INTERROGATION ROOM

[MORRIS *and* DOYLE.]

MORRIS [*reading from a report*]: Papa escorts me to the parlor, where I find three of the children. A girl who looks to be twelve years old playing a perfectly rendered vintage Steinway pianoforte. A five-year-old boy dancing with a dandified guest. And the little girl I saw in the foyer—the one whose cheek Papa was stroking—sitting in a window seat. *What is your name?* I ask. She replies, *My name is Iris.* Without further discussion, she takes my hand and leads me up a grand staircase to the second floor.

We move down a darkened hallway, doors on both sides and the walls covered with weapons. From behind one door come the low sounds of what must be a fourth child, whimpering. Iris leads me to the last door off the hallway. Hanging above it, covered in dark red stains, is an axe.

We enter a bedroom with flowered wallpaper and a white lace bed. A little girl's dream. I case the joint in frank amazement, the detail of rendering—down to the smell of mulch rising from a garden beneath her window—throwing me into a state of pleasure and confusion. Iris beckons to me . . . *Why don't you come here? I won't bite . . .* She then circles her fingers around the bunny's ear, stroking from base to tip—

DOYLE: Okay.

MORRIS: Okay what, Mr. Doyle?

DOYLE: Do you think you're going to shame me into helping you? I'm past shame.

MORRIS: Then why are you finding it hard to listen?

DOYLE: Because I'm sick of your voice. How old are you?

MORRIS: Why do you ask?

DOYLE: You remind me of my students. So full of themselves. So sure they know what the hell is going on.

MORRIS: I'll shut up if you give me the information I need on Papa.

DOYLE: I don't have information. We are anonymous to each other. I have no idea who he is other than how he presents himself in the Hideaway.

MORRIS: Does your wife know about him?

DOYLE:

MORRIS: Why don't we log in right now and contact her.

DOYLE: Fine.

MORRIS: Fine?

DOYLE: My wife won't leave me.

MORRIS: Your daughter?

DOYLE: I've saved enough money for her to finish college. And I don't care what she thinks of me. She's an adult now. She can think any thoughts she wants.

MORRIS: Your job?

DOYLE: Puh. I was considered one of the top teachers in the country, an inspiration to future scientists. I turned down professorships to stay in the public system. I won awards. Then came the Single School Act, which consigned all lessons to educational games in the Nether. I became no more than a monitor, making sure the students weren't hacking through the school firewall to engage in porn.

MORRIS: Is that how you discovered the Hideaway?

DOYLE: The advertising was compelling, to say the least. I wanted to see if they'd gotten it right with Victorian-era inventions.

MORRIS: When you entered, were you aware of your proclivity?

DOYLE: What proclivity?

MORRIS: Little girls.

DOYLE: The image of a little girl.

MORRIS: It's more than that, Mr. Doyle. It's sound, smell, touch. The Hideaway is the most advanced realm there is when it comes to the art of sensation.

DOYLE: Our bodies are ninety-nine percent space. Physical sensation is inconsequential.

MORRIS: As a scientist, how can you say that? Sensation is our gateway.

DOYLE: Yes? Gateway to what?

MORRIS: To understanding the rules of the world.

DOYLE: The world we walk upon. But what about the world of our imagination?

MORRIS: Exactly the same. People meet as physical beings in the Nether.

DOYLE: But there are no longer physical barriers to that contact. Now we may communicate with anyone, through any form we choose. And this communication—this experience of each other—is the root of consciousness. It is the universe wanting to know itself. Can't you see what a wonder it is that we may interact outside our bodies? It's as revolutionary as—discovering fire!

MORRIS: And just as dangerous. Who are we when we "interact" without consequence? What is revealed by feeling an axe slide through the flesh of a little girl?

DOYLE: The revelation is when she resurrects and comes to stand before you again. Images, sensations—those are fleeting. It's the relationships that matter.

MORRIS:

DOYLE:

MORRIS: You intend to cross over. I thought your affairs were in remarkable order. Of course you're not concerned with anything in-world. You were going to become a permanent shade.

DOYLE:

MORRIS: That is an egregious step, Mr. Doyle. And still highly experimental. You've probably looked into life-support systems. I can tell you from experience they're not half as good as they're advertised. I've seen bodies, after only one year, that are unrecognizable.

DOYLE: This bag of flesh is unrecognizable.

MORRIS: We treat shades here. It is a long battle to get them to accept themselves again. The suicide rate is high. We have programs—

DOYLE: I don't want your programs.

MORRIS: The desire to live as someone else is a symptom of depression.

DOYLE: I'm not depressed. I'm sad.

MORRIS: What about your in-world relationships? What about your daughter?

DOYLE: I'll tell her where to find me.

MORRIS: So she can come visit? A nice little family visit in the Hideaway?

DOYLE: We could stroll arm in arm down a country lane . . .

MORRIS: Do you think Papa would allow that?

DOYLE: She would need to obey the rules of the realm, but absolutely.

MORRIS: Our agent didn't find Papa so magnanimous. In fact he reports a rigid behavioral prescription—

DOYLE: Your agent listed facts in his report. But the next time you have a chat by the water cooler, don't ask him, *What did you see? What did you do?* Ask him, *How free did you feel?*

SCENE 6
IRIS'S BEDROOM

[IRIS *stands with her stuffed rabbit as* WOODNUT *inspects the room.*]

WOODNUT: This bedroom. It's beautiful. A little girl's dream.

IRIS: I'm glad you like it, Mr. Woodnut.

[*He goes to the window.*]

WOODNUT: Sunshine. Warmth. Is that a garden down there?

IRIS: Snap peas. Swiss chard. Lemon basil.

WOODNUT: Is it seasonal?

IRIS: Absolutely. You are fortunate to visit us in late spring.

WOODNUT: Four seasons . . . adding up to a year?

IRIS: We don't think of it as "adding up." Nothing here truly changes.

WOODNUT: And whose idea was all of this?

IRIS: Papa's, of course.

WOODNUT: Papa? He is not merely a chaperone?

IRIS: Oh no, he created the Hideaway.

WOODNUT: He came up with the idea? And did the programming?

IRIS: We don't use that word here, Mr. Woodnut.

WOODNUT: I apologize.

IRIS: It is your first time.

WOODNUT:

IRIS: Why don't you come here? I won't bite.

[*She circles the bunny's ear with her fingers, strokes it from base to tip.* WOODNUT *clears his throat. He approaches her.*]

IRIS: It's okay to be nervous.

WOODNUT: I'm not nervous.

IRIS: Go ahead then. Touch me.

[WOODNUT *pats her stiffly on the head. She takes his hand and moves it over her face. He jerks his hand away.*]

IRIS: Perhaps you'd like to start with the axe.

WOODNUT: I beg your pardon?

IRIS: That usually comes after, but if you're more inclined that way—

WOODNUT: No. No. I do not wish to start with the axe.

IRIS: Alright.

WOODNUT: Is it—expected?

IRIS: Papa prefers it for returning guests, but we don't have to do it the first time. Is there something else you'd like to play? I've got marbles, jacks, pick-up sticks . . .

WOODNUT: What are those?

IRIS: They are games. I can show you. How about jacks?

[IRIS *pulls a bag of jacks out of her dress pocket and kneels down on the floor. She motions* WOODNUT *over.*]

IRIS: First I'm going to drop all the jacks. [*She does.*] Now, I'm going to bounce the ball, pick up a jack, and catch the ball again, with the same hand. [*She does.*] See? [*Again.*] Would you like to try?

[WOODNUT *kneels.* IRIS *hands him the ball.* WOODNUT *clumsily bounces the ball, pecks at a jack. The ball goes bouncing off.* IRIS *retrieves it, laughing.*]

IRIS: You were close! Try again!

[*Intrigued,* WOODNUT *gives the task his full attention. He snags a jack and catches the ball.*]

WOODNUT: Aha!

IRIS: Very good! My turn!

[IRIS *scoops up two jacks, catches the ball.*]

WOODNUT: You took two of them!

IRIS: First you take one, then two, then three!

WOODNUT: Let me try.

[WOODNUT *scoops up two jacks, catches the ball.* IRIS *claps.* WOODNUT *laughs, pleased with himself.*]

IRIS: You did it!

WOODNUT: I did it!

[*He suddenly stops, drops the ball, stands.*]

IRIS: Is something wrong?

WOODNUT: I have quite . . . forgotten myself.

[*He goes to the window, stands in the sunlight and shadows of leaves.*]

IRIS: It's okay to do that here, Mr. Woodnut. It's okay to forget who you think you are.

[IRIS *lifts her dress over her head and stands in her knickers.*]

And discover who you might be.

WOODNUT:

IRIS:

[WOODNUT *slowly moves toward her.*]

SCENE 7
INTERROGATION ROOM

[MORRIS *and* SIMS.]

MORRIS [*reading from a report*]: I approach the little girl and fold her into my arms. Her skin is covered in goosebumps, which quickly fade in my embrace. [*Looking up*] The next section of the report is classified, but our agent did collect the evidence we needed to pursue this case. He confessed to me in person this experience left him traumatized.

SIMS: Your agent. Who was he?

MORRIS: That's not important. What's important is—we know everything that goes on in your "establishment." And I have been eager for this encounter, Mr. Sims, so I could ask: How can you, in good conscience, infect people with this content?

SIMS: People come to my realm of their own free will.

MORRIS: They're enticed by its beauty. By sensations they can no longer experience in the real world.

SIMS: Is it my problem the real world no longer measures up?

MORRIS: I would say it's all of our problem. But who's going to do anything about it when they're busy molesting children?

SIMS: What are you afraid of? Violence? Porn? Did you know porn drives technology? The first photographs? Porn. The first movies? Porn. The most popular content when the Nether was called the Internet? Porn. The urge, Detective—the *urge*—as long as we are sentient, you will never stamp that out. You must have spent time in those collegiate fantasy realms . . . questing . . . killing wicked demons and wild boars. And the sex . . . I've been there . . . I've seen the cock bulges. In-world men are no comparison, with their soft, interface hands. Don't tell me you never fucked an elf.

MORRIS: No, Mr. Sims, I never fucked an elf.

SIMS: Come on, you're missing out. The point is—it doesn't matter whether you kill a boar or a demon. Whether you have sex with a child or an elf. It's nothing but images. And there is no consequence.

MORRIS: Images—ideas—create reality. Everything around us—our houses, our bridges, our wars, our peace treaties—began as figments in someone's mind before becoming a physical or social fact.

SIMS: Are you accusing me of creating pedophiles? If anything, I'm giving them a place to blow off steam.

MORRIS: You foster a culture of legitimization, telling them their desires are not only acceptable, but commendable. Do you know what your guests are doing in-world?

SIMS: Do you? I've read the studies. No one has been able to draw a conclusive correlation between virtual behavior and actual offense—

MORRIS: There won't be a distinction when everyone decides they'd rather cross over. We are at the edge of what could become a mass migration into the Nether.

SIMS: Is that my fault, too?

MORRIS: Your code is the closest anyone has come to perfecting the art of sensation—

SIMS: My code?

MORRIS: Spend enough time in the Hideaway, and you forget—

SIMS: You want my code.

MORRIS: —you want to forget the world itself—

SIMS: You want to sell it to Disney.

MORRIS: No, Mr. Sims—

SIMS: Use it to create some insipid realm where you can brainwash users into buying crap they don't need.

MORRIS: We give our users more credit than that.

SIMS: You track them like bloodhounds. Now you want to tell them what to do. Or rather, what not to do. What not to think. What not to feel.

MORRIS: You said yourself—the Nether is becoming our contextual framework for being. If that happens, the same laws should apply—

SIMS: It's not the same way of being! It's imagination! People should be free in their own imagination! That is one place, at least, where they should have total privacy! I grant them that. The Hideaway's identity encryption is so profound, even I don't know who comes in. You couldn't have hacked it without my knowing . . . how on earth did you find me?

MORRIS: There is a line, even in our imagination. You don't just offer images of children. You provide the sound and the smell and the touch of them.

SIMS: You found me through one of my users . . .

MORRIS: Even the eyes look alive.

SIMS: One of my guests, one of my children . . .

MORRIS: They believe themselves to be real.

SIMS: Iris. She started asking questions. After spending time with . . .

MORRIS: They even believe your love for them is real.

SIMS: Mr. Woodnut! He's your agent. He got to Iris. What did he do to her?

MORRIS: It's what you did to her, Mr. Sims. And I assure you, there's been a consequence.

SCENE 8
IRIS'S BEDROOM

[*Music spills from a gramophone.* WOODNUT *is in his shirtsleeves.* IRIS *stands on his feet. They waltz.*]

IRIS: One two three, one two three. Left foot three. Right foot three. Left foot three. Right foot three . . . you're getting it!

WOODNUT: Don't say that—you'll mess me up!

IRIS: You're doing better, Mr. Woodnut. Much better than last time. And vastly improved since we started.

WOODNUT: It's the dancing shoes. I bought them with my returning guest credit.

IRIS: It's also you. You're starting to feel it. Can't you tell?

WOODNUT: Yes . . . yes . . .

IRIS: I do believe you're a natural . . .

[*The music ends.* WOODNUT *spins her around. She shrieks with delight. He puts her down and she wobbles.*]

IRIS: Whoa! I feel . . . I feel . . .

WOODNUT: Dizzy?

IRIS: Happy!

WOODNUT: Me too!

[*They beam at each other. Then a slight nervousness comes over* WOOD-NUT. *He takes the record off the gramophone and holds it up.*]

WOODNUT: Where does the music come from?

IRIS: From the grooves. Can you feel them?

WOODNUT: Why yes. Yes, I can. But how are they turned into sound?

IRIS: You place the needle at the edge, and it follows what is actually a single groove that spirals all the way to the center of the record, picking up vibrations.

WOODNUT: How do the vibrations get there?

IRIS: The reverse process. A sound is made, and they are etched into a master record.

WOODNUT: And then how do we hear them again?

IRIS: They go through the needle and hit a diaphragm at the base of the horn, which amplifies the sound.

WOODNUT: My goodness! It's all hardware!

[IRIS *clears her throat pointedly.*]

WOODNUT: I beg your pardon—I mean—it's all mechanical!

IRIS: Yes, it is!

WOODNUT: It's incredible what we have done using the materials of the earth. Not only have we built roads and cities, but we have created tools for our imagination.

IRIS: It's like magic.

WOODNUT: Exactly. Although I think we must be careful about letting the magic sweep us away, to the point where we forget where it came from. I personally like to have these . . . materials . . . to hold onto. Something tangible. I don't know what happens when the music plays, but I like being able to touch the grooves. Even when it comes to people.

IRIS: People?

WOODNUT: Yes. I may feel a certain way about someone and think they feel the same way about me, but how do I know it's mutual?

IRIS: Don't you trust the feeling?

WOODNUT: Not entirely. Take Papa, for example.

IRIS: What about Papa?

WOODNUT: You care for him a great deal.

IRIS: I do.

WOODNUT: Does he feel the same way about you?

IRIS: Of course.

WOODNUT: How do you know?

IRIS: Because of what he shares with me.

WOODNUT: What he shares with you here. But it's easy here. I only bring this up because, you see, my father was more interested in the world of his imagination than he was in me—

IRIS: Mr. Woodnut! Sharing personal details is—

WOODNUT: —against the rules—I know. But sometimes you go out of bounds with someone you care about. Let me just say, even if he had invited me into his world, even if we had danced together in the beautiful music of our minds, what I needed most from him, what I felt would truly express his love, was entrusting me with something—even a small thing—that was real.

[IRIS *mulls this over, troubled.* PAPA *enters.*]

PAPA: Iris, have you forgotten our afternoon together?

IRIS: Oh! Is it afternoon already?

PAPA: Yes, it is. Mr. Woodnut, you've quite gone over your time.

WOODNUT: Have I now? Iris, you should have told me.

IRIS: I forgot.

PAPA: You forgot?

IRIS: We were having fun.

PAPA [*flustered*]: Well, don't let me interrupt—

IRIS: Wait, Papa!

[*She goes to* PAPA, *puts her hand in his.*]

IRIS: Thank you, Mr. Woodnut. That will conclude our time.

SCENE 9
INTERROGATION ROOM

[MORRIS *and* DOYLE. DOYLE *is weary, resigned to the questioning.*]

MORRIS: I gather from our agent's report it was forbidden for members of the Hideaway to give out information about their real lives.

DOYLE: Correct.

MORRIS: Did anyone, as far as you know, break the rules?

DOYLE: No.

MORRIS: Papa? Did he ever break the rules?

DOYLE: No.

MORRIS: Are you sure?

DOYLE: I'm tired.

MORRIS: Mr. Doyle, I must ask you to sit up.

[DOYLE *straightens, resentfully.*]

MORRIS: So. You first came to the Hideaway as a guest?

DOYLE: Correct.

MORRIS: How did you choose to appear?

DOYLE: Younger. I had thick hair the color of wheat.

MORRIS: At what point did you become close to Papa?

DOYLE: Almost immediately. Sometimes I'd go to the Hideaway just to visit with him.

MORRIS: What would the two of you do?

DOYLE: Play billiards. Drink cognac. Talk.

MORRIS: What did you talk about?

DOYLE: Industrialization. The amazing steam engine.

MORRIS: So this was all in character?

DOYLE: If that's how you need to frame it.

MORRIS: But inventions were a popular topic?

DOYLE: Yes.

MORRIS: And what did the two of you deduce?

DOYLE: About what?

MORRIS: Human invention? Progress?

DOYLE: That we are trying to cast off the limitations of physicality and become pure spirit.

MORRIS: Is that how you see crossing over? Becoming pure spirit?

DOYLE: Something like that.

MORRIS: But Papa's realm demands form. A set of prescribed looks.

DOYLE: The guests may choose from a wide range of appearance selections.

MORRIS: What about the children? Do they have a choice?

DOYLE: The children are employees.

MORRIS: What about Iris? Was she there when you arrived?

DOYLE: No. Another little girl.

MORRIS: Another little girl?

DOYLE: Henrietta.

MORRIS: Did she look like Iris?

DOYLE: Yes.

MORRIS: Even though someone else was behind her?

DOYLE: Of course.

MORRIS: So all of the children, no matter who is behind them, look the same.

DOYLE: The guests enjoy continuity.

MORRIS: That sounds like something Papa would say. Who was it before Henrietta?

DOYLE: I don't know.

MORRIS: And before her. And before her. Who was the first little girl?

DOYLE: I never asked.

MORRIS: I wonder if she was someone real.

DOYLE: That's pure speculation.

MORRIS: Speculation is my job. What happened to Henrietta?

DOYLE: She went to boarding school.

MORRIS: Boarding school?

DOYLE: That's what . . . Papa said.

MORRIS: Isn't that what happens when children do something naughty? Get sent away?

DOYLE: Maybe her behinder needed to move on.

MORRIS: Maybe she broke the rules. Maybe she got too close to Papa.

DOYLE: All of the children are close to Papa.

MORRIS: But does he have a favorite?

DOYLE: Well, there are always those beings to whom you are particularly drawn.

MORRIS:

DOYLE:

MORRIS: Did you tell Papa about your intention to cross over?

DOYLE: No.

MORRIS: Why not? From the looks of your financial documents, you've been prepared for months.

DOYLE: It's a big decision. I've needed to deliberate—

MORRIS: Has anyone crossed into the Hideaway? Children or guests?

DOYLE: I don't know.

MORRIS: Has Papa?

DOYLE: I don't know.

MORRIS: Was he ever gone when you logged in?

DOYLE: He could have been somewhere else in the Nether, doing business—

MORRIS: But wasn't the topic open for discussion? If you're part of Papa's big, happy family, wouldn't he want to have at least some of you there all the time?

DOYLE: You weren't there. You don't know how it works—

MORRIS: You've been there for years—why haven't you once brought it up? Unless you're not so sure of his response. Unless you're secretly afraid that if you offer yourself up to him, he'll punt you off to boarding school—

DOYLE: Look, you can do the hard-boiled baloney on me all you want, but I know—I *know*—what's in his heart!

SCENE 10
A SUNNY SPOT

[PAPA *and* IRIS *sit beneath a vault of trees. The sound of leaves fluttering is heard. Beside* PAPA *is a huge box.*]

IRIS: . . . and Barnaby said Antonia shoved him. And Donald wasn't saying anything because his shorts were dirty too. The thing is it was Antonia's idea all along. She wanted to find out if the eggs *feel* warm when they've just come out of the chicken, and I said why didn't you ask me—I could have told you they do. And she said just because I'm Papa's favorite doesn't mean I should put on airs, and I said I'm not your favorite. Look how after the spanking room you kept stroking Donald's face and gave him that candy that's only for guests!

PAPA: Why do you get jealous?

IRIS: Not me. Antonia.

PAPA: I mean all of you. Don't you believe there's enough affection to go around?

IRIS: Maybe.

PAPA: Love is not like a sack of corn. You don't run out of it the more you give away.

IRIS: I know.

PAPA: And you can't believe everything she says. You are too trusting, my dear.

IRIS: Isn't that something you like about me?

PAPA: I just want you to be careful.

IRIS: I know.

PAPA [*humored*]: *I know, I know* . . . you know everything, don't you?

IRIS: I know I must be a little bit special, to get to spend an afternoon with you.

PAPA: Well, of course you are special. It seems one of our guests has noticed it, too.

IRIS: You mean Mr. Woodnut?

PAPA: You've been spending quite a bit of time with him.

IRIS: He's fascinated by what you've done here. He asks all kinds of questions.

PAPA: What does he ask?

IRIS: About you and how everything works.

PAPA: About me?

IRIS: I can't say I don't encourage him.

PAPA: Has Mr. Woodnut availed himself of the axe?

IRIS: I don't think he's inclined in that direction.

PAPA: He's a returning guest. Perhaps you should give him a nudge.

IRIS: Shouldn't we let guests come to things on their own time?

PAPA: It keeps them from getting too close. That's something you should watch, as well. It makes you vulnerable and could upset a balance.

IRIS: Are you jealous?

PAPA: Iris!

IRIS: I'm just teasing, Papa. You know you're my favorite.

PAPA:

IRIS: Did you bring me something?

PAPA: Maybe.

IRIS: Is it a birthday cake?

PAPA: Let's call it an Iris Day cake.

IRIS: I want to see!

[*He lifts the cover. The cake is beautiful, multitiered. It looks like glass.*]

IRIS: Oooooooooo!

PAPA: It's made of ice that will never melt.

IRIS: I can hear it. It's the sound of freezing and unfreezing.

PAPA: The cake reforms its crystal patterns.

IRIS: And there's another sound. The sound of tiny dwarves who live in snowy mountains singing falsetto. Can you hear it?

PAPA: No. I can't. It must be only for children to hear.

IRIS: Is that why you don't want me to grow up?

PAPA: Why?

IRIS: Because I'll no longer hear the singing?

PAPA: Because I don't want to lose you.

IRIS: It wouldn't be good for business.

PAPA: That's not why. You know why. Don't you?

IRIS: I feel it, but . . . I do sometimes wonder if it's real.

PAPA:

IRIS:

PAPA: Come here, Iris Day Girl.

[*She scoots closer.*]

PAPA: Did you know these trees are called poplars?

IRIS: Yes.

PAPA: No you didn't!

IRIS: Yes I did!

[*He tickles her. Overlapping "No you didn't!"/"Yes I did!" as they giggle.*]

IRIS: I promise! I did!

PAPA: Okay, I believe you! So here's a secret: I have a garden.

IRIS: Our garden?

PAPA: No, my own garden.

IRIS: What's in it?

PAPA: The same things that are growing in ours. And guess what I just planted? I've scoured the world for it.

IRIS: What?

PAPA: A sapling. A poplar.

IRIS: That's real?

PAPA: Real real.

IRIS [*moved*]: Thank you.

PAPA: Don't tell the others.

[*She shakes her head emphatically. They sit for a moment, listening to the wind in the leaves.*]

PAPA: There were poplars growing by our vacation cottage. It was the last grove in the country. I would wake to my bedroom wall aglitter with sunshine, the sound of wind washing through the leaves, and my mother at the window. She said, *The only way you hear the wind is if it has leaves to blow through.*

IRIS: I miss the trees.

PAPA: I do too.

IRIS: I love you.

[PAPA *hesitates.*]

SCENE 11
INTERROGATION ROOM

[MORRIS *and* SIMS.]

MORRIS: You cultivate a parade of little girls, each looking like the one before. You let them get close, but not too close. When they start expressing real emotion, it's off to boarding school.

The guests choose from a set of looks that you provide. The children look the same, no matter who's behind them. The way everything appears is completely under your control.

You create a realm irresistible to anyone with a longing for beauty, go there each day, play the music, pull the strings, and force everyone else to dance to your nightmare.

SIMS: I don't force anyone to do anything. Your agent—Woodnut—knows that.

MORRIS: It's here in the report. What you made him do.

SIMS: He got close to a little girl. He had sex with her. That's a highly illegal act for a member of law enforcement, but perhaps the Nether community has deemed it permissible?

MORRIS: In the interest of collecting evidence—

SIMS: He could have collected evidence in one visit. He kept coming back.

MORRIS: He needed more information.

SIMS: He came back because he liked it.

MORRIS: He followed protocol and conducted a successful operation. Your presence here is proof of that.

SIMS: I think he even fell in love with Iris. He brought her flowers . . .

MORRIS: Why do the girls look the same?

SIMS: And then she started asking about the other little girls . . .

MORRIS: Iris. Henrietta. They're always the same and always your favorite.

SIMS: She was gone for three days . . . she came back and she was— crying—

MORRIS: Who was the first little girl? Was she someone real?

[SIMS *suddenly moves toward her.*]

SIMS: Tell me what happened to Iris.

MORRIS: Give me the location of your server.

SIMS: What did you do to her?

MORRIS: Give me the location, and I'll tell you what your psychosis has wrought.

SIMS: *My* psychosis? What is all of this to *you*? You clearly abhor shades. Maybe Mummy and Daddy spent too much time online and didn't pay enough attention to you? Personal insecurity draws you to law enforcement. Rookie detective, finds a home with "an investigative unit of the Nether"—whatever the hell that is. Some shadow group that's got a few thugs, an interrogation facility, and the entire population by their short and curly logins. And so pure you never even fucked an elf. Have you ever fucked anything, Detective? In-world or otherwise? [*reaches for her*] Have you ever been—

MORRIS: Don't touch me.

[*He stops.*]

We don't repeat

MORRIS: You don't know what I've done. And don't position yourself as someone who's protecting Iris. I don't know who the first little girl was, or what you did to her, but using her image revictimizes her over and over again. Your concern is an act. Like Papa's kindness is an act. There is no love in your realm. There is only your ego. You even look like yourself in the Hideaway. And if people don't do what you want, you—

SIMS: How do you know what I look like in the Hideaway?

MORRIS:

SIMS:

MORRIS: Our agent made a positive ID.

SIMS: You made a positive ID.

MORRIS: No, Mr. Sims—

SIMS: Oh, yes. We had a chat over cognac. I recognize you.

SCENE 12
THE HIDEAWAY FOYER

[*Late-afternoon sun pours through the window.* WOODNUT *enters, whistling. He wears a fancy new jacket and carries a bouquet of flowers. He preens in a wall mirror.* PAPA *enters, carrying an axe.* WOODNUT's *joviality evaporates.*]

WOODNUT: Papa.

PAPA: Good afternoon, Mr. Woodnut.

WOODNUT: I have a visit with Iris.

PAPA: She's been delayed by another guest.

WOODNUT: I see.

PAPA: It seems you're not the only one who favors her.

WOODNUT:

PAPA: Cognac?

WOODNUT: Um. Certainly.

[PAPA *casually puts down the axe, goes to a side table, pours two glasses of cognac, hands one to* WOODNUT.]

PAPA: Cheers.

[*They drink.*]

WOODNUT: Oh my. This is strong.

PAPA: Aged fifty years.

WOODNUT: How do you do it?

PAPA: Perfecting this world is my obsession.

WOODNUT: Do you think obsession is required?

PAPA: For perfection?

WOODNUT: For making the world as you think it should be.

PAPA: Oh yes.

WOODNUT: I tend to agree. To what do I owe the honor of a drink?

PAPA: You've taken a shine to Iris. I've taken a shine to you.

WOODNUT: She's winsome.

PAPA: She's the best I've found.

WOODNUT: The best . . . of what?

PAPA: Suffice to say that all of one's children are cherished, but sometimes there is a favorite.

WOODNUT: I'm treating her quite well, if that's what you're concerned about.

PAPA: It is my concern. You should be careful about getting attached.

WOODNUT: This is merely a diversion.

PAPA: You visit quite a bit for a mere diversion. And I've noticed you've not yet [*indicating the axe*] proceeded with the relationship.

WOODNUT: Is that entirely necessary?

PAPA: For returning guests, it shows a desire to partake fully of what we offer here.

WOODNUT: And what is that?

PAPA: A life outside of consequence.

WOODNUT:

PAPA: Is that not something you can subscribe to, Mr. Woodnut?

WOODNUT: It is something I find hard to believe is possible. You see, my father was a shade . . . I beg your pardon. The cognac is having an effect.

PAPA: It hits hard if you're unaccustomed to it. But go on.

WOODNUT: I'm afraid I may break the rules.

PAPA: This one time, I give you leave.

WOODNUT: He never looked at me when I was a child. He never touched me. He never took me outside. All I remember is his body on life support, curling up. When he died, he listed me as the beneficiary of his login. I entered the Nether as him and found a single realm—a small room with an armchair and a fire. Over the mantle was a round mirror with my reflection, a wizened gargoyle. On a table next to the chair was a book of poems by Theodore Roethke, with one passage highlighted:

> Dark, dark my light, and darker my desire.
> My soul, like some heat-maddened summer fly,
> Keeps buzzing at the sill. Which I is I?
> A fallen man, I climb out of my fear.

The mind enters itself, and God the mind,
And one is One, free in the tearing wind.

[*A challenge.*]

PAPA:

WOODNUT:

PAPA: I see why Iris likes you.

[*He downs the rest of his cognac.*]

> Mr. Woodnut, you have been asking questions about me. I must request you desist. And unless you want me to consider your activities here suspect, I suggest you . . . move along with the program.

[*He puts one hand on* WOODNUT'*s arm, fatherly, and holds the axe out to him with the other.*]

PAPA: Maybe this will help you climb out of your fear.

SCENE 13
IRIS'S BEDROOM

[*Evening now.* WOODNUT *stands before* IRIS *with axe and flowers.*]

IRIS: It's okay, Mr. Woodnut. I always resurrect.

WOODNUT: I don't want to do this.

IRIS: What are you afraid of?

WOODNUT: Will it hurt you?

IRIS: I feel only as much pain as I want.

WOODNUT: How much pain is that?

IRIS: That's rather a personal question.

WOODNUT: It's so beautiful here. Why do we have to bring in something terrible?

IRIS: Beautiful. Terrible. It's like life.

WOODNUT: Except that it isn't.

IRIS: It's an opportunity to do something you could never do otherwise.

WOODNUT: I have already been with you in ways that—

— are there universal morals, even outside "reality"?

54

IRIS: That's one side. This is the other. Creation. Destruction. You begin to realize they're on the same wheel.

WOODNUT: I've interacted with some of the other guests. This technique does not seem to have set them on a path to enlightenment.

IRIS: People come to things on their own time. We offer a place where you may dismantle everything the world has told you about right and wrong and discover pure relationship. *seems like she's trying to change what's*

WOODNUT: I don't think this is Papa's plan. I think it's yours. *right/wrong irl*

IRIS: That's not true. He created this place—

WOODNUT: Papa did not create this place to foster pure relationship. I think you've made that up to justify wanting to stay here.

IRIS: Mr. Woodnut!

WOODNUT: He does not love you.

IRIS: He does!

WOODNUT: You think because you feel love, so does everyone else—

IRIS: It's not just a feeling! He gave me something.

[WOODNUT *jerks.*]

WOODNUT: What did he give you?

IRIS: Just like you said. He told me something real.

WOODNUT: Something from his real life?

IRIS: Yes! I asked him, and he told me.

WOODNUT: What was it?

IRIS: I cannot tell you.

WOODNUT: You must. You must tell me what he said.

IRIS: I cannot tell a soul.

WOODNUT: Don't you trust me?

IRIS: Of course I do. And Papa trusts me.

WOODNUT: He doesn't trust you, he controls you. He controls everything! He sits at his terminal and makes you dance at the end of his strings!

IRIS: That's not true! And I must remind you of the—

WOODNUT: —rules! Yes, all of the rules here! Rules about saying too much! Rules about getting too close! It's supposed to be about freeing yourself, and yet nothing is truly free—

IRIS: Mr. Woodnut, I would kill myself if I betrayed him!

WOODNUT: Okay. Okay. I cannot make you see.

[*He flings himself onto the window seat and sulks.* IRIS *mulls. Finally:*]

IRIS: I cannot give you Papa's offering. But I can give you one of mine.

WOODNUT: Isn't that against the rules?

IRIS: Yes.

WOODNUT: Alright.

IRIS: I won a Distinguished Teaching Award in Theoretical Physics.

WOODNUT:

IRIS:

WOODNUT [*earnest*]: Congratulations.

IRIS: Thank you.

WOODNUT: Thank *you*.

[*She gives him a long hug. He touches his eyes. Startled to find them wet. He jumps up.*]

WOODNUT: I think I understand why Papa wants this. It's so we don't get too attached. And maybe he's right. Maybe I should not get too attached. → does it hurt to know Iris isn't real / is trapped?

[*He retrieves the axe, turns to* IRIS.]

WOODNUT: Come here.   •how much is Woodnut being controlled?

SCENE 14

INTERROGATION ROOM

[MORRIS *and* DOYLE.]

MORRIS: And in those moments, standing in the carnage of her small body, the hot smell of everything we have inside rising around me, I stare at the blood on my hands and think, my god, look at the brightness of it, look at the bright beauty, how does this exist in nature, how does it exist in any way, in any code I can understand? I look down to find her body gone. What have I done, have I done something, have I done nothing, is this all nothing, is everything nothing? A giggle at the door, and she reappears, coming toward me with her arms open—and I lift the axe and do it again. And I do it again. And I do it again. I want her to stop coming so I know I've done something. But she keeps coming, and now it's not just my hands covered in blood, it's my face, it's my body, I can taste it in my mouth, it's so exquisite I am crying, I have never felt so much with every nerve, felt so much, felt so much . . . feeling. Until I'm spent. And she comes to me again, eyes wide. But if there has been no consequence, there has been no meaning—no meaning between her and myself, between myself and myself—and if there *has* been meaning, then I am a monster.

[DOYLE *looks at her hard. His mouth drops.*]

DOYLE: It was *you* . . .

DOYLE:

MORRIS:

DOYLE: . . . the Physics Award . . .

MORRIS: We investigated previous winners until we found someone with an excessive login time and an off-shore bank account.

DOYLE: How could you do this to me? After everything we—

MORRIS: I'm doing this for you.

DOYLE: You're deeply disturbed if you think this is helping—

MORRIS: Deeply disturbed doesn't begin to cover my state of mind after what I—

DOYLE: You didn't have to do it. Any of it. You could have left us alone.

MORRIS: The Hideaway is wrong.

DOYLE: It draws people who are—broken—I know that, but—I don't judge them—they are part of us, too—they are part of the world— God does not judge them—why should we? →universal morals, again

MORRIS: You fell into a relationship—it's emotional—I understand—

DOYLE: Do you? Do you understand?

MORRIS: This man you call Papa does not feel for you as you do for him.

DOYLE: I know he does.

MORRIS: He's obsessed with an image he created.

DOYLE: It's more than that.

MORRIS: Whose idea was it that you transition from guest to little girl?

59

DOYLE: Papa's.

MORRIS: He could only become intimate with you in that form.

DOYLE: No! I had—spent all of our money. It was a way for me to stay in the Hideaway.

MORRIS: He'd been grooming you. He doesn't want a relationship, he wants control. I was there—I know this—murdering children does not keep you detached, it makes you complicit!

DOYLE: You don't know anything! He gave me something real.

MORRIS: What was it?

DOYLE: I'm not telling you! You may have me, but you won't get Papa.

MORRIS: He had something real to give you! Something from his real life. He doesn't live in the Hideaway—he's not crossing over— why would you?

DOYLE: I don't want to be here anymore.

MORRIS: What about your daughter? Have you really told your daughter?

DOYLE: She is an adult now—I am not responsible—

MORRIS: You are! You are responsible to her forever!

DOYLE: I'll tell her where to find me—

MORRIS: In the Hideaway? My father was a shade, and what I wanted most from him was a relationship here on this earth!

DOYLE:

MORRIS:

DOYLE: I trusted you.

MORRIS:

DOYLE:

MORRIS: Mr. Doyle, you have been the greatest surprise of my professional life. You are my . . . first love, if you can imagine that. I believe what Papa's doing is wrong—it's hurting you—but I'm willing to put it to a test. I will let you see him again. If he loves you—*you*—and wants you to cross, I'll let you stay in the Hideaway together. If not, you will give me what you have on him.

DOYLE:

MORRIS: This is the offer I'm allowed to make. I'll stake my career on it. Take it, or you'll never see him again. And then how will you know what's in his heart?

DOYLE:

MORRIS: Come, Mr. Doyle, let's log in.

[MORRIS *and* DOYLE *become . . .*]

SCENE 15
IRIS'S BEDROOM

[. . . WOODNUT *and* IRIS. *She is shivering.*]

WOODNUT: Are you cold? Would you like me to—

IRIS: No. Don't touch me, Detective.

WOODNUT: He's coming. I'll be right here.

[WOODNUT *hides.* PAPA *enters.*]

PAPA: There you are, my child! Where have you been?

IRIS: I have had a fever.

PAPA: For three days?

IRIS: I'm afraid so.

PAPA: Why didn't you send me word?

IRIS: Papa, I have to ask you a question.

PAPA: Of course.

IRIS: The girls before me. Like Henrietta.

PAPA: What of them?

IRIS: Did you feel about them the way you do me?

PAPA: I don't understand.

IRIS: Why do we all look alike?

PAPA: You know the guests enjoy continuity.

IRIS: The guests, Papa? Or you?

PAPA: Are you being impertinent?

IRIS: Who was the first?

PAPA: The first what?

IRIS: The first little girl? Was she someone you knew?

PAPA: Iris. In a moment of affection, I gave you a small piece of something real, but asking this of me—you go too far.

IRIS: I'm sorry, Papa.

PAPA: You know we have rules here.

IRIS: I respect the rules. I would live with them entirely. I want to cross over.

PAPA: You want to cross?

IRIS: Wouldn't you like to have me here all the time?

PAPA: I need to remind you this is a business.

IRIS: Is that all it is?

PAPA: No, but objectivity is required to keep us afloat.

IRIS: But am I special to you?

PAPA: Of course. Haven't I made that clear?

IRIS: Am I special, not just as Iris?

PAPA: You *are* Iris.

IRIS: No, I am more than that! I am more than something you've made! Do you love *me*?

PAPA:

IRIS:

PAPA: I don't think you should cross. Take a few days off, come back, and we'll forget this conversation ever happened. If you find yourself unable to forget, it may be time for boarding school.

[IRIS *starts weeping.*]

PAPA: Iris. Iris, stop that. Stop it right now. I did not build the crying function for this purpose. Iris! This is exactly what I am talking about! This is the problem with getting too close! Iris, do as I say!

[*He slaps her. Long pause.*]

IRIS: Mr. Woodnut once asked me if I feel pain. And I said to him, only as much as I want. But I see now, that's not quite the pain he meant.

PAPA [*anguished*]: Is there anything I can do to make it up to you?

IRIS [*slowly*]: You could tell me one more time about your secret.

PAPA: I have a garden, with a poplar. One of the last in the world.

IRIS: Thank you.

PAPA: Certainly.

IRIS: I'm sorry.

PAPA: You don't need to apologize.

IRIS: Yes, Papa, I do.

[*She sniffles, pulls herself together.*]

IRIS: Now if you don't mind, I have guests.

PAPA: Of course.

[PAPA *reaches to touch her affectionately, but she only puts out her hand, businesslike. They shake.*]

PAPA: It is—good to have you back and working.

[*An awkward pause.* PAPA *exits.* WOODNUT *emerges.*]

WOODNUT [*gently*]: You did very well.

[IRIS *stands in an attitude of dejection.*]

WOODNUT: I know that was hard. I'm sorry. I really am.

[IRIS *stands.* WOODNUT *moves to the window.*]

WOODNUT: Once, sitting here, I had a memory of being held up to a window . . . I looked out and, on the horizon, saw the sun coming through a thin line of trees. I'd always assumed I was too young to remember trees. And I'm not sure if, sitting here, I didn't make that memory up. But either way, I must admit, it gives me comfort.

[*He turns to* IRIS.]

I will make sure you and your family are looked after. Everything I said, back in the room, was real.

[IRIS's *only movement is a sort of mechanical breath.*]

WOODNUT: Are you alright?

[*No response. He goes to her.*]

WOODNUT: Iris?

[*He touches her. No response.*]

WOODNUT: Mr. Doyle. Mr. Doyle.

[MORRIS *returns halfway to herself and finds* DOYLE *missing from the interrogation room.*]

WOODNUT/MORRIS: Mr. Doyle!

SCENE 16
INTERROGATION ROOM

[MORRIS *and* SIMS.]

SIMS: What did you do to her?

MORRIS: It's what you did.

SIMS: The last time I saw her, she was crying.

MORRIS: Why was she crying?

SIMS: She was crying because . . . the poplar . . .

MORRIS: Saplings are exceedingly rare. It was easy to track the shipments.

SIMS: You used her to get that out of me.

MORRIS: Mr. Sims, Iris was a sixty-five-year-old man.

SIMS: Stop. We have the right to remain anonymous.

MORRIS: He was a middle-school science teacher with a wife and a daughter.

SIMS: It is unethical for you to reveal—

MORRIS: His name was Cedric Doyle.

SIMS: —to reveal her identity to me!

MORRIS: What are you afraid of? Are you unable to accept him in his true form?

SIMS: That's not her true form—

MORRIS: It is, Mr. Sims. It was.

SIMS: What do you mean—it was?

MORRIS: We brought him here for questioning. After three days we sent him back to the Hideaway to get the information we needed. And then . . . before we knew what he was doing . . . he disengaged from our terminal and hanged himself.

SIMS: What?

MORRIS: With his belt. The day before we brought you here.

SIMS:

MORRIS:

SIMS:

MORRIS:

SIMS: You killed her.

MORRIS: No, you did.

SIMS: You had sex with her. You liked it.

MORRIS: You brainwashed him.

SIMS: I made a place where she was happy.

MORRIS: His happiness wasn't about the place. It was about you. He thought you loved him.

SIMS: And you told her I didn't.

MORRIS: I let you do that.

SIMS: You don't know what's in my heart!

MORRIS: Do you?

SIMS: I meant everything I said to Iris. I—cared—

MORRIS: Would you have cared about him as an old man?

SIMS: ~~That wasn't who she was—~~

MORRIS: Yes, that's who he was. He was in the body God ~~gave him~~.

SIMS: God? You stand in this room and speak of God?

MORRIS: As in what we are given. What we are made of. The materials of the earth.

SIMS: Aren't we more than that? Iris said she believed God is how we are with each other.

MORRIS: And how would you have *been* with Mr. Doyle if you'd sat with him in this room?

SIMS: I don't know, because this room, this world, has been so perverted by other people's ideas of what it should be. You and your speeches on images creating reality and why don't we make a better reality—look around! Look at this room. Look at what *you've* created. A place to twist people. A place to terrorize them. What did you do to Mr. Doyle? Did you make him see the truth? Did you bring him to the light? Did you save him? No, actually, what you did was betray his trust, drag him from a place where he felt safe, and submit him to psychological torture until he killed himself.

[MORRIS *looks around the room* ...]

MORRIS:

SIMS:

—isn't it better to live ignorantly or die knowing?
⇒ very Brave New World

69

MORRIS:

SIMS:

MORRIS:

SIMS:

MORRIS:

SIMS: The server is in an anchored sub off the coast of Malaysia. Latitude 4.795417, Longitude 104.567871. The server sitter's name is Jerry. He has no idea what's running on it. Don't hurt him.

MORRIS: Thank you, Mr. Sims.

SIMS: It doesn't matter anymore.

MORRIS:

SIMS:

MORRIS: I didn't like the Hideaway. I loved it. I wanted to stay there forever. I wanted to stay in that beautiful home with Iris. But if I had, who would I have been?

SIMS: Detective Morris. Is that your real name?

MORRIS:

[*She begins to pack up.*]

SIMS: You're not going to return my login, are you?

MORRIS:

SIMS: In-world banishment. How appropriate.

[*She starts to leave.*]

SIMS: There was a real little girl. The daughter of my neighbor down the street. We would get together in person then. All of the neighbors. This was a long time ago. I couldn't stop thinking about her. She had hair the sun played in. And a laugh that came out of her like magic. I wanted to . . . get inside. I pretended to be her friend. I posed to her family as a young, harmless uncle-type. One night I got her alone in her own room. We were laughing, and I reached over and grabbed her, and she looked at me—so startled—and I . . . found it in myself to let her go. I went home, to my computer, and that's where I've stayed. You don't know what you do, Detective, putting me out into the world.

MORRIS: The world is still the place we have to learn to be. You are free to go, Mr. Sims. You are free.

[*She exits, leaving* SIMS *alone.*]

(handwritten annotations:)
very contradictory

— pedophilia is extreme, but what about the recent beginning of accepting homosexuals? In the past, they would have to "learn to be" what society expected of them.

EPILOGUE

[SIMS *and* DOYLE.]

DOYLE: Did you bring me something?

SIMS: Maybe . . .

DOYLE: Is it a birthday cake?

SIMS: Let's call it an Iris Day cake. It's made of ice that will never melt.

DOYLE: I can hear it. It's the sound of freezing and unfreezing.

SIMS: The cake reforms its crystal patterns.

DOYLE: And there's another sound. The sound of tiny dwarves who live in snowy mountains singing falsetto. Can you hear it?

SIMS: No. It must be only for children to hear.

DOYLE: Is that why you don't want me to grow up? Because I'll no longer hear the singing?

SIMS: Because I don't want to lose you.

DOYLE: It wouldn't be good for business.

SIMS: That's not why. You know why. Don't you?

DOYLE: I feel it, but . . . I do sometimes wonder if it's real.

SIMS:

DOYLE:

SIMS: Come here, Iris Day Girl. Did you know these trees are called poplars?

DOYLE: Yes.

SIMS: No you didn't!

DOYLE: Yes I did!

[*Overlapping "No you didn't!"/"Yes I did!" as they giggle.*]

DOYLE: I promise! I did!

SIMS: Okay, I believe you! So here's a secret: I have a garden. And guess what I just planted? A sapling. A poplar.

DOYLE: That's real?

SIMS: Real real.

DOYLE: I miss the trees.

SIMS: I do too.

DOYLE: I love you.

[SIMS *hesitates.*]

SIMS: You cannot know how much I love you.

END hm.

PRODUCTION NOTES

It is recommended to cast Iris with an actress who will appear on stage as a prepubescent girl. The child actor takes the audience *out* of the play (Bert States, *Great Reckonings in Little Rooms: On the Phenomenology of Theater* [Berkeley: University of California Press, 1987]), which is desirable considering the contents of her scenes. The audience is assured nothing awful will be enacted upon the child, whereas they have no such confidence with an adult posing as a child. A young actress also adds warmth, which is critical to the chemistry of the play.

There are three references that place the play in the United States of America. However, producers should feel free to make the location specific to their country. "Franklin Middle School" should refer to a public school for children around ages eleven to thirteen. "Illinois State University" should refer to a modest, well-established public university. "Brownstone" should refer to an historical urban dwelling, built before 1930, possibly as mass housing during the Industrial Revolution, and now typically inhabited by wealthy urbanites who can afford homes made of natural materials like stone and wood.